Paul Frédéricq

The study of history in England and Scotland

Paul Frédéricq

The study of history in England and Scotland

ISBN/EAN: 9783743346222

Manufactured in Europe, USA, Canada, Australia, Japa

Cover: Foto ©ninafisch / pixelio.de

Manufactured and distributed by brebook publishing software
(www.brebook.com)

Paul Frédéricq

The study of history in England and Scotland

TABLE OF CONTENTS.

7

THE STUDY OF HISTORY
IN
ENGLAND AND SCOTLAND.

In April, 1884, the University of Edinburgh celebrated its
three hundredth anniversary with a festival not soon to be
forgotten by those who had, as I had, the good fortune to be
present.

I took the opportunity that a trip to Scotland afforded, to
observe the methods of advanced instruction in history in
that country, and, afterward, to pursue the investigations in
England, before returning to Belgium. M. Van Humbeck,
our late minister of public instruction, entrusted this task to
me in order to complete the information gathered on my two
previous missions, in 1881 and 1882, to Germany and Paris.[1]

I.—UNIVERSITIES OF SCOTLAND.

Scotland has four universities : Edinburgh, Glasgow, St.
Andrew's and Aberdeen.[2] The first is particularly flourish-
ing, and is noted for its Medical Faculty.[3]

---

[1] See author's articles *De l'Enseignement supérieur de l'histoire en Allemagne*
(*Revue de l'instruction Publique en Belgique*, Vol. XXIV, pp. 18–53, and
Vol. XXV, pp. 79–92) and *De l'Enseignement supérieur de l'histoire à Paris*
(*Revue internationale de l'enseignement*, Paris, July 15, 1883, 61 pages).

[2] In round numbers there were at these four universities in 1884: At
Edinburgh, 3,300 studen's; at Glasgow, 2,000; at Aberdeen, 900; at St.
Andrews, 250.

[3] I visited only the universities of Edinburgh and Glasgow, whose management is excellent and whose corps of professors counts, especially at Edinburgh, savants of European reputation.

9

I was astonished to find that history is in reality excluded from the curriculum of Scottish universities. At Aberdeen and St. Andrew's it has not the slightest notice, save cursorily in the department of Latin, Greek, and English literature. At Edinburgh and Glasgow there is a single course, called "Constitutional Law and History," that is taken only by law-students, and is a course in jurisprudence rather than in history. But the fact that at Edinburgh the professor in charge of this department, Mr. J. Kirkpatrick, wears the title, Professor of History, marks a little progress and implies hope for the future.

Mr. Kirkpatrick, who kindly furnished me these details, arranges his course in constitutional law and history—chiefly English—as follows: he requires of his pupils, who are law-students, four recitations and one hour of written work, each week during the summer term. The subjects treated are the points the professor has discussed, in relation to which the pupils have read indicated portions of such well-known authors as Stubbs, Hallam, May, Freeman, Molesworth, Gneist, and Guizot.

I give, as illustrations, the questions used in two of these written examinations.

First examination, Wednesday, 23d May, 1884: 1. What is the domain of constitutional law? 2. Describe briefly the political organizations of the Anglo-Saxons about the middle of the eleventh century. 3. How does the feudalism established by William the Conqueror differ from the feudalism of the Continent? 4. What were the chief articles of the charter of Henry I.? 5. How were the evils of feudalism aggravated during the reign of Stephen? 6. What were the principal stipulations of the Constitutions of Clarendon?

Ninth and last examination, Wednesday, 21st July, 1884: 1. Enumerate the rules of constitutional law contained in the Bill of Rights (1689) and in the Act of Settlement (1701). 2. Give the history of religious toleration in England from

the time of William III. to 1858. 3. How was the pro-
cedure in trials for high treason reformed under William III.
and Queen Anne? 4. Give a brief outline of the question
of exclusion of place-men from Parliament between 1701 and
1782. 5. Mention some characteristic acts proving the auto-
cratic disposition of George III., and relate briefly the affair
of Wilkes. 6. Name and explain briefly the consequences
that followed the passage of the Reform Act in 1832, and
show concisely the reforms effected by that law.

These written exercises are evidently mere repetitions of the
professor's lectures. He corrects the papers and marks and
ranks the students according to their merit. At the end of
the term a prize, consisting of books, is given to the best two,
and the names of all that have obtained at least seventy-five
points out of one hundred are published in a rank-list. The
professor also suggests one or two subjects for essays to be prepared independently. Prizes are awarded for the best of these.
About thirty students choose this course.

At this elementary stage there can be no question of studying sources and inculcating methods of scientific research. The
most that can be done is to inspire the desire of reading certain
text-books and great works relating to the history of English
constitutions. The easy written examinations at regular inter-
vals keep the students on the alert, but do not urge them to
individual research. They belong more properly to elementary teaching.

This incomprehensible exclusion of history from Scottish
universities cannot continue. A new act of Parliament is in
preparation which will enlarge the roll of the Faculty; let
us hope that history will thus obtain the recognition it receives
in the universities of all civilized countries, and which it long
ago deserved in the country of Robertson, Walter Scott and
Carlyle.

II.—Cambridge and Oxford.

No university on the Continent can impress the visitor as do time-honored Cambridge and Oxford. The two towns are scarcely more than villages like Göttingen; but the noble monuments of learning that abound there would furnish architectural glory for great cities. The English-Gothic style shines there in all its splendor. Where is it possible to find, save perhaps at Bruges or Nuremberg, such a cluster of masterpieces of secular mediæval architecture? And to their picturesque grandeur the charming gardens, parks stocked with deer and meadows dotted with venerable trees add enchanting beauty.

Whole streets are lined with handsome structures, the colleges or halls, most of them as large as the great *Lycées de Paris*. There are twenty-four at Oxford[1] and at Cambridge seventeen, each of them possessing a fine garden, a chapel that is often a handsome church, a noble dining-hall, a library often very rich, and one or several interior courts. In several of the colleges of Gothic style, these courts are bordered by cloisters, rivalling the most celebrated on the Continent; they would befit a monastery of the Middle Ages, but no monks are to be met there. Students and professors go to and fro in the morning, their heads covered with black, square-topped caps ornamented with a silk tassel,[2] like a Polish lancer's cap; they wear smartly over their jackets a gown of black woolen stuff,[3] which suggests the flowing mantle of the seventeenth century, and is still the ceremonial costume of professors in

[1] At Oxford there are twenty-one colleges properly so-called and three halls, smaller and less important than the colleges.

[2] At the Norwegian University at Christiana the students wear a black head-gear of the same kind with the long silk tassel. At least such was the dress of their deputies whom I saw in 1877 at the fourth centennial celebration of the University of Upsala.

[3] At Cambridge I saw also blue gowns. At Glasgow the toga was of a bright red.

Belgium and Holland; but the English gown is shorter and
more convenient than the latter, being made of lighter material.

After luncheon at one o'clock, all these learned caps and
grave gowns disappear.   In the gardens and through the
streets of the town in every direction rove the students, in
the gay costume of their college or club.   The English student,
faithful to the golden maxim, *mens sana in corpore sano*, devotes at least two hours a day to physical exercise in the open
air.   In winter he plays foot-ball; in season he rows, plays
cricket, tennis and lawn-tennis, or takes long excursions by
carriage, on horseback, or perched on his bicycle, the vehicle
being furnished at night with a little lantern and a gong for
the benefit of pedestrians.

It is necessary to have seen these handsome young fellows,
tall, slender, supple, muscular, browned by exposure, bending
rhythmically to their oars or returning with vigorous stroke
the white lawn-tennis ball, in those wide gardens with their
carpets of fresh green unknown to us, in the shade of oaks,
beeches and lime-trees older and more majestic than the noblest
on the continent—it is necessary to have admired this goodly
youth, in order to pity adequately the students of other countries, shut into great dirty cities, poorly lodged, rarely taking
long walks, finding recreation only in heated ale-houses reek-
ing with tobacco-smoke and stale odors of beer and alcohol.

In the evening the English students again put on their
square caps and their gowns, to dine with their fellows and
tutors in the college refectory,[1] usually a handsome Gothic

---

[1] Each student takes breakfast and luncheon in his own rooms, which
consist of a good-sized study, a small sleeping-room, and a lumber-room
called at Oxford the "scout's hole," and at Cambridge the "gyp-room."
There is one servant for every six students, who takes care of the rooms
and brings the meals.   I visited the rooms of a student at Pembroke College,
Oxford.   There were a few books in sight, cards of invitation encircling the
mirror, portraits of famous actresses, and three silver cups won in the athletic
contests so high in favor with the youth beyond the Channel.   It was evidently not to the room of a "reading man" that chance conducted me.

hall, ornamented with historic portraits and emblazoned windows.[1] After this repast they go to their rooms or those of friends to spend the evening, or to society-rooms, where the principal journals and reviews are to be found.[2] They never set foot in an alehouse. They return at nine o'clock to their college, being subject after that hour to a fine. By entering but a minute late they are exposed to severe penalties.

Each college is under the management of liberally payed officials, chosen from among the most distinguished men the university has produced. This is especially the case with the director or master. His assistants, called tutors, have oversight of the conduct of the students; they likewise have direction of the written examinations, indicate the books to be consulted and the courses to be pursued, give out written exercises, give private lessons, and even provide courses of study to supply deficiencies in the regular course.

The tutors thus relieve the professors of the tedious and exacting preparations of examination-papers. Free from this care the professor arranges his instructions as he thinks best. At Oxford he gives from time to time a state lecture, at which the Masters, ladies, and the public are present. As a rule he teaches as do the professors of the College of France, at Paris,

---

[1] This dinner is very elaborate. I dined twice with the tutors at Balliol College. The *menu* consisted of two dishes of fish, two of meat, and dessert. They drank at choice beer, ale, sherry, port, bordeaux. Continental students have no idea of such daily feasting. It is well to add that parents pay about £200 a year for their sons' living at Oxford and Cambridge, although the vacations are very long. Poor students are exempted from such expense and live at about £80 a year. They are called "unattached students." They are the exception; at Oxford they number from 200 to 300 out of the 2,500.

[2] With Mr. Arthur Evans, son-in-law of Prof. Freeman, I visited the "Union" at Oxford, a general society of the students. I found a handsome lecture-hall, a smoking-room, restaurant, a room for writing and a large debating-room, in which are held public discussions always closed by vote. It is a true club, well-organized upon a larger scale than the principal aristocratic societies of Belgium.

without being restricted to a special course. The college, however, could not be more watchful over the pupils entrusted
to it; for its reputation is at stake, surrounded as it is by
numerous and no less ambitious rivals.

And here the point at issue is not simply academic rank :
the richest universities, Oxford and Cambridge, which have
an annual revenue of about £600,000,[1] confer each year by
examination numerous scholarships and fellowships. The
former are for undergraduates alone. Those who secure them
are very proud of the honor, and wear a longer gown than
their fellows. These scholarships, which vary from £40 to
£100, and are granted for three, four, or even five years,
materially lessen the burdens of parents. The fellowships
are contested by young scholars who have finished their
academic course, and wish to devote themselves to science.
This is an admirable system, since it puts the man of letters
above the consideration of income, and enables him to live
for science alone. Sometimes an honorary title of fellow is
conferred upon a noted scholar in order to give him pecuniary
freedom appropriate to his rank. Thus Max Müller is a
fellow of Oxford. The same support was recently given by
Oxford to Mr. S. R. Gardiner, to allow him to devote all his
time to his remarkable History of England from 1642 to 1649.
The fellowships are secured for several years or for long
terms, and are worth £150 to £200 or £300 annually.

For scholarships especially there is hot rivalry among the

---

[1] I give the following approximate estimate of Oxford's income in 1877:
£16,800 from rent of real estate and similar sources; £20,000 from students'
fees; £3,000 from the University press, etc. The total cannot be far from
£35,000 or £40,000. In this estimate are not included the incomes of the
twenty-four colleges, which are appropriated; e. g., Balliol £6,000 to
£7,000, Merton £18,000 to £20,000, New College £30,000 to £33,000, Christ
Church £40,000 to £45,000. There must be much useless expense and
squandering that has nothing in common with science in order to dispose
of such fabulous sums. "Much waste," was a word I heard repeated again
and again.

colleges. At Oxford, I was assured, the Balliol men are distinguished for taking high rank. A host of men conspicuous
in literature and in politics have gone out from this college;
such are Sir Stafford Northcote, leader of the Tories, Cardinal
Manning, Lord Chief Justice Coleridge, the poet Swinburne,
Matthew Arnold, Dean Stanley. Parliament boasts thirty
Balliol men.

In short the colleges have far more to do with making the
men than has the university. It may almost be said that
this latter term is but a conventionality of academic speech,
as Metternich used to contend that Italy was only a geo-
graphical expression.

Oxford and Cambridge seemed to me unsurpassed for har-
monious development of body and mind. They send out men,
gentlemen, in the highest sense of the noble word. As regards
scientific organization, I imagine these two universities to be
the College of France, enlarged by numerous college halls,
responsible for the liberal training of its pupils. The colleges
thus closely resemble the Belgian Faculties, which are chiefly
professional schools, but with this difference, that the students
in England do much more independent personal work.

III.—HISTORICAL INSTRUCTION AT CAMBRIDGE.

Until late years history has been crowded to the background
as well at Oxford as at Cambridge. From time immemorial
the latter university has put mathematics before all else, and
Oxford, the branches relating to classic antiquity, especially
the ancient languages. History, which enters only indirectly
into these two specialties, was singularly neglected.

More than a century ago George I. founded at Cambridge
a chair of modern history, whose incumbent is still called
Regius Professor.[1] The head of the House of Hanover had

---

[1] At Cambridge and Oxford the chairs bear the name of their founder,
who is also entitled professor.

in view the education of public officials and diplomatists. But more than once this chair has been filled by historians, it is true, but men who diligently took their ease in teaching history. The place was thus held for years by the poet Gray, who never gave a lecture and whose position as royal professor of modern history was a sinecure, though a very meagre honor, it appears, for his literary merit. For the last twenty years historical instruction has taken a more serious turn, especially since Mr. J. R. Seeley has filled the chair of modern history. This eminent publicist, author of several striking books anonymously published, such as " Ecce Homo " and " Natural Religion," is one of the wisest and most original political historians of contemporary England.[1] He has had a marked influence at Cambridge.

In this university the examination system is a series of severe tests, called triposes, which occur every spring. At first this examination turned chiefly on mathematics, preëminently the science of Cambridge. In 1824 a second tripos was instituted for Latin and Greek, in 1851 a third for moral science and a fourth for natural sciences, and in 1856 a fifth for theology. Then came the turn of jurisprudence, to which was attached modern history, beginning at 1870. Finally a separate tripos for universal history was instituted in 1875.

In four of the seventeen colleges of Cambridge special lecturers[2] are provided to prepare the students for the historical examination. They are: at Trinity College, Mr. B. E. Hammond; at King's, Mr. O. Browning and Mr. Prothero; at Trinity Hall, Mr. Thornley, and at St. John's, Mr. Tanner. Three years are spent in reading for this examination, for which the degree B. A. is conferred. The same degree,

---

[1] Those of his historical works best known on the Continent are: Life and Times of Stein, Germany and Prussia in the Napoleonic Age (3 vols., 1878), and The Expansion of England (1884).

[2] These lecturers have incomes varying from £150 to £300. There are also private tutors who make a living from their lessons.

2

equivalent to a doctor's degree,[1] can be taken in the other triposes, each student choosing his specialty.

The historical tripos[2] is as follows. The examination bears upon English history, including that of Scotland, Ireland, the British Colonies and their dependencies; upon certain indicated parts of ancient, mediæval and modern history; upon the principles of political economy and the theory of law; upon English constitutional law and history of the English constitution; upon public international law in connection with detailed study of certain celebrated treaties; finally, a thesis must be written upon a subject chosen from the ten proposed.

This course was arranged according to the suggestion of a council held in 1873, which formulated its conclusions in these terms: " The council is of the opinion that history, considered as a specialty with a separate tripos, ought to be constructed on a larger scale than when it was merely an accessory to other examinations. Therefore it is proposed to assign to ancient and mediæval history a place in the tripos coördinate with that held by modern history, so that the subject may be presented as a scientific whole.

" It is proposed also to unite each branch of history with one of the principal sciences that depend upon it."

As I have said above, the preparation for the historical tripos requires three years. As a rule the three years are thus employed. The first is devoted to general English history, to economics, and to a special subject of ancient history. The second year is employed in reading part of the history of the English constitution, political economy, and a special sub-

---

[1] The title of Doctor or Master of Arts is obtained without examination at least three and a half years after graduation. A tax of about £20 is paid and the candidate appears before the chancellor of the university to be proclaimed M. A. with traditional ceremonies scrupulously observed.

[2] See "The Student's Guide to the University of Cambridge," Part IX, Historical Tripos (Cambridge, 1882); and Cambridge Examination Papers (Easter Term, 1883, CLXXI. Easter Term, 1884, CLXXXIX, Cambridge, 1883 and 1884).

ject of the Middle Ages.   During the third year the history
of the constitution is finished and the remaining time given
to international law, to political and juridical philosophy, to
a special subject of modern history and a special subject of the
history of international treaties.

· Mr. B. E. Hammond, M. A., fellow of Trinity College,
who has carefully drawn up recommendations for students of
history,[1] insists upon the following points : "The student shall
take with extreme care the college lectures that bear upon the
special subjects indicated for theses ; for if he lose one of these
lectures, it will be, as a rule, impossible for him to obtain any
help in preparing that part of his subject ; the lecturer will
not repeat his readings and it is not to be supposed that anyone
else has studied the subject enough to furnish the same information.

"In addition to those lectures specially intended to prepare
for examination, the student will attend, so far as he can, during the three years, the lectures of the royal professor of history—Mr. Seeley."

The author then goes on to give in detail the books to be
consulted.   As this part of Mr. Hammond's directions shows
the character of the examinations, I think well to transcribe
it here.

"For English history," he says, "it will be impossible to
give a list of works that will apply uniformly to all students;
for a man, who before entering the university is not familiar
with the outlines of English history, will not find time to read
more than J. F. Bright's 'History of England' and Green's
'Short History of the English People.'"   Those, on the contrary, who have learned the general facts in their previous
reading will be able to extend their research at the university.
It is impossible to acquire a satisfactory knowledge of English
history by reading one or two authors ; in all cases, a part of
this reading ought to precede entrance to the university.   It

[1] See his Article in Student's Guide to the University of Cambridge, 1882.

is rare to meet a student who on entering Cambridge pos-
sesses the general knowledge contained in the above-men-
tioned books; but this rare man has a great advantage over
his fellows. He can immediately begin serious study and
combine constitutional with general history. To a student
thus prepared the following list of works will be useful.

I. For the Anglo-Saxon period: Lappenberg's "Anglo-
Saxon Kings," translated from the German; Freeman's
"Norman Conquest," chap. III, and "Old English History," by the same author. II. For the period between
the Norman Conquest and the revolution of 1640 : Lingard's
"History of England" (combined with some other author,
as, for example, Mackintosh on the Reformation); Stubbs'
"Constitutional History," chapters IX to XIII, "Documents
illustrative of English History," and Hallam's "Constitutional History" to chapter XV. III. For the period following the English revolution: Macaulay; Stanhope's "Reign
of Queen Anne;" the reigns of George I and George II
in Stanhope's "History of England" (Mahon); Massey,
"George III;" Miss Martineau, "History of Peace" (the
introduction); and for the corresponding history of the English Constitution, Hallam, chap. XV and XVI; and Erskine
May, "Constitutional History."

As to the history of Scotland, Ireland, and the English
colonies with their dependencies, the parts that pertain directly
to the history of England would naturally first demand the
reader's attention. General notions will have been already
furnished by the works just given. It is, however, fitting to
mention here the best authorities for certain periods of the
modern history of the United Kingdom; thus, for Scotland,
Burton's "History of Scotland" from 1689 to 1748; for the
colonies in their past and present circumstances, Bancroft's
"History of the United States," and Heeren's "Manual of
the Political History of Europe and her Colonies" (translated).

For political and juridical philosophy: Aristotle, "Politics;"

Guizot, "Histoire de la Civilisation en Europe;" Tocqueville, "Old Regime;" Stuart Mill, "On Representative Government;" Freeman, "History of Federal Government" (introduction); Justinian, "Institutes;" Gibbon, "Decline and Fall of the Roman Empire," Chap. XLIV; Austin, "Province of Jurisprudence Determined" (lessons V and VI); Maine, "Ancient Law;" J. F. Stephen, "General View of the Criminal Law of England;" Savigny, "System des Heutigen Römischen Rechts," Vol. I, Bk. I and II, Chap. I. There is one translation of this work by Guenoux, entitled "Traité du Droit Romain." Considerable extracts are also to be found in English in Reddie, "Inquiries in the Science of Law," 2d edition.[1]

For constitutional law and history of the English Constitution: Blackstone, "Commentaries" (Book I, Chap. II to XIII; Book II, Chap. IV to VI; Book III, Chap. III to VI; Book IV, Chap. XIX and XXXIII); Stubbs, "Select Charters;" Hallam; Erskine May; Guizot, "Histoire de la Civilisation en France;" Bryce, "Holy Roman Empire."

For political economy and economic history: Smith, "Wealth of Nations" (ed. McCulloch, Bk. I, Chap. I, V, and X; Bks. III and IV); Mill, "Political Economy;" Brentano, "On the History and Development of Guilds and the Origin of Trade Unions" (translated); Leone Levi, "History of British Commerce;"[2] Baxter, "National Income," "The Taxation of the United Kingdom," "National Debts."

---

[1] This reference to the French translation of a German work is explained by the fact that a knowledge of German is very rare among English students, although French is familiar enough to many of them. I have been told that out of every three students at Oxford, one is likely to be reading a French book; while, on the contrary, only one out of fifty can do as much with a German book. Nevertheless, few of those who read French read with sufficient ease to consult freely the French authors. At Cambridge the situation is practically the same.

[2] Mr. Cunningham's recent work, "The Growth of English Industry and Commerce," is also used.

For international law: Wheaton, "International Law" and
"History of International Law."

Mr. Hammond supplements this long and interesting enum-
eration by these general remarks: "It is possible that some
students will read entirely through each of the books in the
above list. It is certain that all will do well to read many
of them thus; but each man ought to judge for himself how
much he can do. Upon this point no one can give advice of
universal application, except that every student ought to read
through the book in hand, at risk of sacrificing others. Individual predilections and biasses alone can determine what one
should read and what neglect.

"For the special subjects prescribed in the curriculum for
each year, the Board recommend no authors; the students can
get advice from the respective lecturers."

These special subjects are chosen and published in advance.
The following are the subjects of three successive years: For
1882—Greek history, from 776 to 479 B. C.; history of
France, 1302 to 1494; history of England, 1649 to 1714;
history of international treaties, 1648 to 1721. For 1883—
Roman history, 509–290 B. C., including the political institutions of the empire; history of Western Europe, 476 to 800,
including relations with the Eastern Empire; English Reformation, 1509–1560; history of treaties, 1648–1697. For
1884—Greek history, 510 to 403 B. C.; history of Italy,
1250–1494; history of England, 1603–1660; history of
treaties, 1697 to 1763. For the subjects of the last year
the students had to consult especially, Grote, Sismondi, Gardiner, Ranke ("Englische Geschichte," translated), Koch, and
Schœll ("Histoire abrégée des traités de paix entre les puis-
sances de l'Europe, depuis les traités de Westphalie, 15 vol.,
1817).

All regulations of the history examinations are determined
by a special board, called "Board for History and Archæology," which was instituted about ten years ago and is par-
tially renewed every year. The members are elected by

alumni.[1]   At present this Board consists of the royal professor, Mr. Seeley, and of Mr. Hammond, Mr. Browning, Mr. Prothero, Mr. Thornely and Mr. Tanner, the five lecturers in history.

The tripos is a severe test.   It may not last less than five consecutive days, and takes place in May of each year.   The competitors assemble in a large hall and do their work in writing.   I give below the paper for 1884.[2]

On Monday, May 26, the candidates had already, between the hours of nine and twelve, answered nine questions in Greek history, and in the afternoon, between one o'clock and four, they had to answer nine out of these twelve questions :

1. "It is a fact that some men are free and others slaves: the slavery of the latter is useful and just"[3] (Aristotle, "Politics," I, 15).—"We hold this truth as self-evident; that all men were created equal" (Declaration of Independence of the United States).   What arguments can you bring to support these two assertions?   Show to what extent it is possible to reconcile them.

2. Show briefly the necessity and the nature of the reforms instituted by Justinian in his legislation.

3. The epoch of heroic kings is followed by the epoch of aristocracies (Maine).   Prove this statement from Roman history and from the history of a nation of the West or North, showing the part played by these aristocracies in the development of laws.

4. Guizot considered feudalism a species of federal government; weigh the arguments in favor of this view and compare feudalism with other ancient and modern confederations.

---

[1] The Regius Professor is a member *ex officio.*   At Cambridge and Oxford the graduates meet from time to time and take action upon all questions of organization.   It was this body who voted in 1884 by a large majority for the admission of women to the academic examinations at Oxford.   The universities profit by the salutary principle of self-government which is at the base of everything in that happy country.

[2] See Cambridge Univ. Examination Papers, Easter Term, 1884.

[3] The Greek text of Aristotle was given.

5. Consider the causes of the universal growth of towns during the twelfth century and determine to what ex⬛the revival of Roman institutions can be seen therein.

6. According to the principles of Austin, what are limits of rights of subjects against their sovereign and of the sovereign against his subjects? Discuss the application of these principles to the struggles of James I. against Parliament.

7. Show that the following laws are not laws in the true sense of the word : Lynch law, canonical law, the law of cricket and the law of supply and demand.

8. Show how the penal code has been from time to time adapted to occasion and give examples borrowed from the history of the law of treason.

9. Show, with examples from history, what influence public opinion can have on government in countries that have neither democratic nor representative institutions.

10. Distinguish by the aid of ancient and modern authors, between the different methods that can be applied to the study of politics and compare their advantages.

11. What is the meaning of the terms national will and national conscience, as differing from the wishes and opinions of the citizens? Show the importance of these terms in view of the development and rank of states.

12. Weigh the advantages and disadvantages of the different modes of electing executive power in democratic states.

The choice of these questions is remarkable ; it presupposes great cleverness on the part of the pupils; but I question whether when the candidates have but three hours before them, the required answers to nine of these points are not of necessity superficial and mechanical.

On Tuesday, the twenty-seventh of May, the contestants had to treat in the morning nine questions on Italian history, chosen from the period between 1250 and 1494; in the afternoon they had to answer nine out of twelve questions on English history.

On Wednesday, the twenty-eighth, they had but one examination lasting from nine o'clock till noon. This was the day dev███ to the essay, in which the pupil must show his origin█ ▐power. He must choose and treat in detail one only of ◗following subjects:

1. The condition of labor in ancient, mediæval and modern times.

2. The difficulty of administering State lands.

3. The reasons why it is necessary to obey Law.

4. The possibility of a federation between England and her colonies.

5. Thucydides and Clarendon.

6. The connection existing between the political greatness of a nation and its literary greatness.

All these questions involve at the same time history, politics and even philosophy. They illustrate the tendency of historical instruction at Cambridge. It is moreover the essay that constitutes the most important part of the historical tripos and has the most decisive influence upon the student's rank.

On Thursday, the twenty-ninth of May, the candidates had to write upon nine out of the following twelve questions on international law:

1. What influence has the establishment of diplomatic relations among the European states had upon international law and politics? Show the limits to the prerogatives of foreign ambassadors between 1697 and 1763.

2. Define neutrality. What is meant by permanent neutrality? Is it recognized by international law? Explain the connection between the right of asylum and the duty of neutrals.

3. What are the conditions requisite to render valid in the sight of international law grants of territory? What is meant by government *de facto?*

4. Explain the terms *jus postliminii, jus avocandi, droit d'aubaine.* Develop the maxim, *Ut mores gentium mutantur et mutatur jus gentium.*

5. " D'après un usage barbare, dont le cabinet de Londres

s'est plus d'une fois rendu conpable, l'amiral Boscawen atta-
qua le 18 juin 1755, sans qu'il y eût en déclaration de guerre,
deux vaisseaux de guerre française."[1]   Is this accusation
against the English government supported by fact?   What
was the custom established between the European nations
and the United States during the last century, and in this
century in regard to a declaration previous to commencement
of hostilities?

6. Name, with their dates and the wars that they have ter-
minated, the great European treaties that were confirmed by
the treaty of Paris in 1763.   What were the principal com-
mercial treaties concluded during the first part of the eighteenth century?

7. Indicate with precision the successive phases of the
Great Alliance.   What were the pledges that bound the members when negotiations for peace were opened in 1711?

8. How far were religious interests involved in the war of
the Spanish succession?   Can you cite examples of guaranties
formulated in favor of religious claims in the treaties concluded
between 1697 and 1763?

9. It has been said that Russia entered in 1717 the alliance
of European nations.   Criticize this statement.   Were any
improvements in the foreign policy of Russia accomplished
during the ten years following?

10. What was the import of the Pragmatic Sanction of
Charles VI and the Family Compact of 1761?   Point out
some historical analogies to these two agreements and sketch
the history of the Pragmatic Sanction up to the beginning of
the first Silesian war.

11. In what circumstances did the war of the Polish succession break out and by what arrangements was it closed?
Discuss the imputations that have been made against those
arrangements.

---

[1] This reference was given in French, from what historian I do not know.

12. Trace, through the history of treaties, the successive phases of England's foreign policy between the peace of Aix-la-Chapelle and the commencement of the Seven Years' War; do the same for Russia from this war to the peace of Huberts-bourg.

Nine out of twelve questions in political economy and history of economics had to be answered in the afternoon of the same day. These questions dealt with the great problems of political economy; with the substitution of machines in place of manual labor, with excess of production, with the fluctuations of population in their effects upon wages and rents, with free trade, with the colonial system ancient and modern, with the former condition of farming classes in England, with industrial legislation and the trades, with capital, with the economic effects of war, etc. These questions were in almost every case so arranged as to demand accurate knowledge of history.

Friday, May 30, 1884, was the last day of the historical tripos. In the morning the candidates had to answer nine questions on the history of England between 1603 and 1660. The last question was this: " Discuss the importance and value of the following works: Baillie's ' Letters,' Clarendon's ' History,' Rushworth's ' Collections ' and Whitelock's ' Memorials.' " Then in the afternoon again nine questions out of twelve, relating to English constitutional law and its history were set with this restriction, that at least two of the last three questions be answered. Some bore upon the interpretation of fragments of ancient texts taken from Stubbs' Select Charters (the Great Charter, for instance); others required the discussion of certain assertions made by Hallam, etc. These were the last three: 10. Trace the origin of the Parliament of Paris and of the States General, and show the changes in them under the absolute monarchy. 11. Ranke (*Weltgeschichte*, I, 354) has compared the Athenian revolution of 411 B. C. to that of the Italian republics in the fourteenth and fifteenth centuries. Explain this comparison. 12. What were the political relations existing among the English colonies in North America before the War of Independence and what was the attitude of these colonies toward England?

Surely five days of examination could not be more crowded! The historical tripos, combining to a certain extent the substance of a fellowship-examination in French history with such an examination as that of the free school of political science at Paris, presents a formidable appearance, and seems no less than overwhelming. It demands of the students knowledge so varied and extensive that the result must be, in most cases, a mass of superficial notions without a solid scientific foundation. Perhaps I am mistaken, but appearances at least are in favor of this comment.[1] It is evident that this overwhelming historical tripos does not frighten the students at Cambridge, who devote three years to preparing for it. The number of pupils who present themselves steadily increases. In 1876, the first year, only twelve dared face the history examinations; now there are about forty every year.

However hasty and superficial reading the scope of the historical tripos seems to necessitate, the students fortunately have, in Mr. Seeley, a master whose first care is to make them think for themselves. In the university course, which consists of a weekly one-hour lecture, he sets forth, for students of both sexes,[2] subjects well calculated to provoke reflection. For proof one need only read the notes of his lectures for 1881–1882, upon the expansion of England,[3] in which he discussed successively the tendencies of English history, the state of that country in the eighteenth century, the empire, the

---

[1] It should be observed that the candidate is not obliged to answer *all* the questions on the paper, and that in the matter of rank the one must stand highest who answers the greatest number of questions, their merit in other respects being equal. This practice certainly goes far to limit the exorbitant demands of the paper; but the principle of surcharged examinations still remains to be criticised.

[2] There are at Cambridge two colleges especially for women.

[3] The Expansion of England. Leipzig. Tauchnitz, 1884.

old colonial system, the influence of the New World on the Old, commerce and war, the phases of the expansion; the loss of the English colonies of North America, its history and policy; the Indian Empire, how the English conquered and governed it, the influence of England and India upon each other, the phases of the conquest, dangers internal and external, and the conclusion of the whole subject. These lectures are full of deep and original observation. They furnish a sort of philosophy of English history from the seventeenth century.

But it is in his private course, called " Conversation-class," that this able master of political history must exercise the most profound influence. Like Mr. Waitz and Mr. Droysen, in Berlin,[1] Mr. Seeley meets in his study those students that wish to work under his direction. Every Thursday, for one hour in the morning and one in the afternoon, he receives in turn the students of either sex, and discusses with them the principles of historical and political science. Each of these classes numbers about fifteen pupils. Mr. Seeley assured me that the young women took a more lively interest than the young men, because the former are less surfeited with all that pertains to study. The young women are generally about twenty-one years of age. Mr. Seeley had among them in 1884 Miss Longfellow, daughter of the great American poet.

In his conversation class Mr. Seeley has an original method which compels his pupils to think. The first lesson lasts only a few minutes. The professor puts the question, " What is history, and what is its object? " This he requests the class to consider for a week; and after all have thoroughly pondered the problem, in the second lesson the professor first gathers and discusses the various definitions and then gives his own. In the same way through the successive interviews they study other problems growing out of those that have pre-

---

[1] See De l'Enseignement supérieur de l'histoire en Allemagne (Revue de l'instruction publique de Belgique, Vol. XXIV and XXV).

ceded, as: "History being a political science, what is politics?
What is its method? The historical method. The object of
history is πόλις, society, which manifests itself in the phenome-
non of government. The definition and classification of these
societies." Here Mr. Seeley develops his system of classification, the explanation and discussion of which takes several
months. The pupils also present theses upon subjects of their
own choice, which Mr. Seeley examines and submits for discussion in the class-room. He strives to teach his pupils first
of all, not to be satisfied with mere words, nor with approxi-
mations. He teaches them how to form clear and sound con-
ceptions, and how to establish the fundamental truths of history
and politics. He combats vigorously the dogmatism in vogue
with the radical school in England. " I wish," said he to me
with a shrewd smile, " to make political sceptics, because with
us no one feels the slightest doubt in politics at a time when
all the world is in doubt about religion. I often speak to
my pupils of our political parties (Whig, Tory and Radical),
giving their history and criticising their principles. I offend
no one as I take care to speak with German objectivity. As
I grow older, my pupils have more respect for me and do not
question my authority as they did during the first years of my
professorship at Cambridge; but I continually put them questions. I regret that they do not dare to argue with me as
they did ten years ago, when to my delight they would hardly
deny what I upheld. I believe no exercise is as useful as this.
Our English students are not bold enough for work upon the
sources, what the Germans call *Quellenstudien.* Moreover there
is great danger of their losing themselves in much reading,
without forming sound general notions."

For the sixteen years since 1869 that Mr. Seeley has been
professor at Cambridge he has purposed to form citizens and
statesmen, an object to which the university has scarcely otherwise addressed itself. " Look at Gladstone," he said to me.
" At Oxford where he did such brilliant work, they taught
him only Latin, Greek, and Aristotle." Mr. Seeley takes care

also to draw serious students into personal relations with himself. He puts himself at their disposal every evening at six
o'clock, receiving thus on an average one student each day.
This custom recalls the *sprech-stunde*, that admirable tradition
of German universities.

The example set by Mr. Seeley has been followed by
Mr. Browning, lecturer at King's College, who established in
1876 his so-called "Political Society." It is composed of
twelve students, who meet with their master Mondays at nine
o'clock P. M., to discuss questions of political science. At
each of these meetings, usually lasting till eleven o'clock, one
member reads an original essay, upon which all must express
an opinion; the discussion frequently ends in a vote or
resolution. The minutes of each meeting are kept. Mr.
Browning kindly permitted me to look through the last
volume of these records, from which I noted the following
subjects: The socialism of Plato; Is it desirable that England
should be an empire (resolved in the negative by six to four);
The responsibility of James I. in the events of 1640 to 1642;
England's right of seizure by privateers, etc. Mr. Browning
himself had read a paper upon the events which brought about
the triple alliance in 1788, based upon his own researches in
the archives of London and Paris. Such a debating club,
directed by a spirited leader like Mr. Browning, must con-
tribute much to make its members reflect upon questions of
history and speculative politics.

In 1884 a fund of about £1175 10s. was given to the
University of Cambridge, to found in honor of Thirwall a
yearly prize for the student who would present the best treatise
upon some subject requiring orginal research. This Thirwall
prize is the only one at Cambridge within the reach of students of history.

Let me here express my thanks for the valuable hints
obligingly given me by Mr. Hammond and Mr. Browning
and especially by Mr. Seeley, whom I had the honor of meeting at Edinburgh and who showed me the utmost hospitality

at Cambridge. The hours spent with this eminent man will
never be forgotten.

IV.—THE STUDY OF HISTORY AT OXFORD.

The student at Oxford, before becoming eligible for a degree,
undergoes two pass-examinations. The first, in arithmetic,
geometry, algebra, Latin and Greek, he may take even before
entering the university; many take it during or at the end of
the first year. At the end of the first year the second pass-
examination also takes place, the main feature of which is, at
option, the continuations of algebra and geometry or elementary logic; it includes, beside, a more searching test in the
Greek and Latin offered by the candidates (e. g. three books
of Livy or Tacitus; two of Thucydides, or six of Homer, or
Demosthenes on the Crown). The Greek of the four Gospels
must be presented.

After these two preliminary examinations which require
but one year, the students must choose a specialty in which to
take their B. A., as at Cambridge. The various topics of
examinations are taken from the Classics, including also
ancient history in a subordinate position, mathematics, theology,
natural sciences, law and modern history. Until 1870 the last
two topics were in one. History was thus emancipated five
years earlier at Oxford than at Cambridge, the reform at the
latter university having gone into operation only in 1875.

The number of professors and lecturers in history is notably
greater at Oxford than at Cambridge. At Cambridge there
are but one professor and five lecturers; at Oxford there are
two professors, a reader, and thirteen lecturers. At the time
of my visit to Oxford in 1884, the Regius Professor of Modern
History was Mr. Stubbs, who had just been appointed to the
Episcopal See of Chester, as successor to whom had already
been named another well-known scholar, Mr. E. A. Freeman.
The second professor of modern history was Mr. Burrows,
one of the founders of the " Wiclif Society." There was,

besides, a professor of Indian History, Mr. S. J. Owen, having the title of reader. The thirteen lecturers in history connected with the colleges were Mr. Coolidge, Mr. Wakeman, Mr. George, Mr. Bright (Master of University), Mr. Johnson, Mr. Reichel, Mr. Knox, Mr. Boase, Mr. Hassall, Mr. Lodge, Mr. Smith, Mr. Armstrong, and Mr. Johnson.

This large corps of instructors renders possible a very extensive and varied historical course. The departments are as follows: history of Europe during the last part of the sixteenth century, history of England since 1485, historical archæology, the Tudors, history of England since 1553, history of England since 1642, English constitutional history since James II, history of England since 1714, the period following the accession of George IV, history of India in the Middle Ages, history of the British conquest of Mahrattas, history of the East from 1000 to 1328, history of Spain from 1328 to 1519, general history of Europe (periods of 1610–1648, 1714–1740, 1789–1815), etc. To these historical courses is added a course in political economy and governmental institutions (Mr. Marshall), a course in Anglo-Saxon, including study of the laws of Canut (Mr. Earle) and a course in Celtic, in which the professor, Mr. J. Rhys, explains the text of *Táin bó Cúailngne* as it is found in *Lebor nah Uidre*.

This fine array suggests the programmes of the great German universities, where the number of historical subjects is equalled by their variety; but I have been assured that many of the lecturers restrict themselves to a somewhat elementary style of teaching, without reference to sources or original documents, thereby leaving unemployed all the scientific equipment in use beyond the Rhine. Add to this the fact that no practical course crowns all this theoretical teaching at Oxford, at a time when the German facilities could not exist without their numerous *Uebungen, Gesellschaften*, seminaries, etc., where the students are trained in method and in individual research.

Although the classics are the traditional specialty at Oxford, history claims many more followers there than at Cambridge,

3

almost as many as the famous classics themselves. I have been told that about two hundred or two hundred and fifty students work for the history examination. At least two-thirds of them intend merely to gain their bachelor's degree, without cherishing any scientific passion for history. Of the remainder some are young men of noble family, destined for political careers, who look upon history as useful to the states-man; others purpose to become journalists, a career in England almost a science; still others are reading for the bar, and study history for its bearing upon law; the small remainder are to be teachers, and make history the main feature of their pro-fessional training.[1] Thus enlightened regarding the large numbers who elect the history examination at Oxford, we see that very few study history for its own sake.

The department bears the name of "Honour School of Modern History." Beside the first year required for the two pass-examinations before mentioned, two years or two and a half, rarely three, are devoted to this reading. The candidates must know all English history up to 1837, Queen Victoria's accession; all English constitutional history and one special period of English history in detail; a correspond-ing period of universal history; a special subject worked up from original documents; politics and political economy; his-torical geography. The examination consists of four papers on the political and constitutional history of England, two on general history, two on the subject studied in the sources, one on political economy, and one upon geography. Afterward is held a *viva voce* examination. The candidates are ranked by these examinations in four classes and their names are pub-lished in the rank-list. About ten out of a hundred aspirants each year win places in the first class.[2]

---

[1] Still the majority of those who intend to become teachers make their preparation a profound study of the ancient languages.

[2] Here are the four classes for the years 1882, 1883 and 1834: First Class, 4, 10, 11; Second Class, 24, 19, 14; Third Class, 34, 37, 27; Fourth Class,

As some changes have recently been made in this tripos,[1] to take effect in 1886,[2] I will give here in detail the course then to be pursued. Just as for the historical tripos at Cambridge the official programme recommends a great many authors. For politics and political economy the candidates will be examined upon the following works: Aristotle, "Politics;" Hobbes, "Leviathan" (ch. 13–30); Bluntschli, *Lehre vom Modernen Stat* (vol. I); Maine, "Ancient Law;" Mill, "Political Economy." This is, it seems, a little less extensive than the examination at Cambridge, where there is a tendency to make political science take the precedence of history.

For constitutional history the candidates must read the following : Stubbs, "Select Charters" and "Constitutional History;" Hallam and May; Bagehot, "English Constitution." They must also be ready to make comments upon the principal charters.

For general history of England up to 1837, portions of the following are prescribed: Freeman, "Norman Conquest" (ch. 1, 2, 3, 23); Green, "History of the English People" (vol. I); Stubbs, "Constitutional History (especially ch. 10, 12, 14, 16, 18); Ranke, "History of England" (bks. 1, 2, 3, 22); Macaulay, "History of England" (ch. 1, 2, 3); Bright, "History of England" (vol. II, III).

In the wide field of English history which they must have ranged from end to end, one of the following seven periods is to be presented in detail: 449–1087, 802–1272, 1215–1485, 1399–1603, 1603–1714, 1714–1815, 1760–1848.

In general history is studied the period corresponding to the one chosen for English history. The candidate is expressly required to introduce the literary history and that of the

---

42, 32, 25. This makes the total number of history students for each of these years, 104, 98, 77.

[1] The required periods of universal history have rightly been shortened and corresponding periods of English history added.

[2] For all details see Oxford University Gazette (June 3, 1884).

general civilization of his special epoch in connection with
its political history and geography. It is not, however,
expected that original documents will be used, the object
being rather to induce clear and intelligent reading of the
best authors. For this purpose a vast number of books to
be either consulted or read are especially recommended by
the faculty.

Below is the curious list:

HISTORY OF ENGLAND.	GENERAL HISTORY.
449-1087.	**476-1083.**
Kemble, *Saxons in England.*	Gibbon, *Decline and Fall.*
Green, *Making of England.*	Milman, *Latin Christianity.*
" *Conquest of England.*	Fustel de Coulanges, *Féodalité.*
W. Bright, *Early English Church History.*	Guizot, *Civilisation en Europe.*
	Waitz, *Deutsche Verfassungs-Geschichte*
Freeman, *Norman Conquest.*	.· (vol. II).
Skene, *History of Scotland.*	H. Martin, *Histoire de France.*
Anglo-Saxon Chronicle.	Grégoire de Tours (from bk. V).
Laws of Ine, of Alfred and Canute.	Paul Diacre (from bk. III).
Bede (bks. III and IV.)	Sismondi, *Républiques italiennes.*
	Giesebrecht, *Geschichte der Deutschen Kaiserzeit.*
	Finlay, *History of Greece.*
	Muir, *Life of Mahomet.*
802-1272.	**936-1272.**
Green, *Conquest of England.*	Gibbon, *Decline and Fall.*
Freeman, *Norman Conquest.*	Hallam, *Middle Ages.*
Pauli, *Geschichte von England.*	Milman, *Latin Christianity.*
" *Life of Simon of Montfort.*	Guizot, *Civilisation en Europe.*
Palgrave, *England and Normandy* (vol. III, ch. IV.)	Martin, *Histoire de France.*
	Michelet, *Tableau de la France* (bk. III of Histoire de France).
Preface to Roger of Hoveden (II and IV).	Joinville, *Vie de Saint Louis.*
" to Benedictus Abbas II.	Sismondi, *Républiques italiennes.*
" to Roger Bacon.	Geisebrecht, *Geschichte der Deutschen Kaiserzeit.*
" to Walter of Coventry II.	
" to *Monum. Franciscana I.*	Von Raumer, *Geschichte der Hohenstaufen.*
" to *Itinerarium Regis Ricardi.*	
Anglo-Saxon Chronicle.	Busk, *Mediæval Popes, Emperors, and Crusaders.*
Matthew Paris (period of Henry III).	

Skene, *History of Scotland.*
Robertson, Scotland under Early Kings.
Wright's *Political Songs* (pp. 6, 19, 42, 72, 121, 124, 125, ed. by the Camden Society).
Digby, Real Property (pp. 1–56, 122–151, 253–262).

Finlay, *History of Greece.*
Von Sybel, *History and Literature of the Crusaders.*
Church, *Life of Anselm.*
Cotter Morison, *Life of St. Bernard.*

1215-1485.

Lingard, *History of England* (to 1399).
Pauli, *Geschichte von England.*
"   *Life of Simon of Montfort.*
Preface to *Monum. Franciscana I.*
"   to *Edward II.*
Longman, *Life and Times of Edw. III.*
Sharon Turner, *History of England* (since 1399).
Sechler, *Wiclif.*
Fortescue, *De laudibus legum Angliae.*
More, *Rich. III. and Edw. V.*
Paston Letters (preface by Gairdner).
Burton, *History of Scotland.*
Roger, *History of Agriculture and Prices in England* (Vol. I and III.
Wright, *Political Songs* (pp. 6, 19, 42, 72, 121, 124, 125).

1272-1519.

Gibbon, *Decline and Fall.*
Hallam, *Middle Ages.*
Milman, *Latin Christianity.*
Martin, *Histoire de France.*
Froissart, (bk. II, ch. 52–63, 83–102, 121–128, 148–214, 227–230).
Sismondi, *Italian Republics.*
Amari, *War of the Sicilian Vespers.*
Creighton, *The Papacy during the Period of Reformation.*
Von Reumont, *Lorenzo di Medici.*
Vilari, *Savonarola.*
"   *Macchiavelli.*
Ranke, *Geschichte der Römischen und Germanischen Völker von 1494 bis 1514.*
Prescott, *Ferdinand and Isabella.*
Finlay, *History of Greece.*
Yule, *Marco Polo.*

1399-1603.

Sharon Turner, *History of England.*
Paston Letters (Gairdner's Preface).
More, *Utopia, Richard III and Richard V.*
Bacon, *History of Henry VII.*
Froude, *History of England.*
Brewer, Prefaces to *State Papers.*
Herbert de Cherburg, *Life of Henry VIII.*
Burnet, *History of the Reformation* (ed. Pocock).
Knight, *Pictorial History of England* (1588-1603).
Burton, *History of Scotland.*

1414-1610.

Hallam, *Middle Ages.*
Ranke, *History of the Popes.*
"   *History of the Reformation in Germany.*
"   *Civil Wars in France.*
"   *Geschichte der R. u. G. Völker.*
"   *Die Osmanen und die Spanische Monarchie.*
Martin, *Histoire de France.*
Sully, *Mémoires.*
Creighton, *Papacy during the Reformation.*
Von Reumont, *Lorenzo di Medici.*
Robertson, *Reign of Charles V.*

Latimer, *Sermons* (ed. Arber).
Hooker, *Ecclesiastical Polity* (with the preface).
Spenser, *View of the State of Ireland.*
Smith, *De Republica Anglorum.*

Häusser, *Period of the Reformation.*
Prescott, *Ferdinand and Isabella.*
"   *Philip II.*
Helps, *Spanish Conquests.*
Motley, *History of the United Netherlands.*
Finlay, *History of Greece.*
Elphinstone, *History of India* (ed. Cowell).

1603-1714.

Ranke, *History of England.*
S. R. Gardiner, *History of England.*
Clarendon (bk. I–VI).
Christi, *Life of Shaftesbury.*
Macaulay, *History of England.*
Burnet, *History of His Own Times.*
Wyon, *History of Grt. Britain during the Reign of Queen Anne.*
Swift, *Conduct of the Allies.*
Burton, *History of Scotland.*
Sir John Davis, *State of Ireland.*
Doyle, *English in America.*
Bruce, *Annals of the East India Company.*
Dryden (Political Poems).

1610-1715.

Heeren, *Political Systems of Modern Europe.*
Ranke, *Französische Geschichte.*
Martin, *Histoire de France.*
Voltaire, *Siècle de Louis XIV.*
"   *Charles XII.*
De Retz, *Mémoires.*
Ranke, *History of the Popes.*
"   *Die Osmanen u. d. Sp. Mon.*
"   *History of Prussia.*
Coxe, *History of the House of Austria.*
Droysen, *Gustaf Adolf.*
Chapman, *Gustavus Adolphus.*
Montecuculli, *Mémoires* (bk. II, III).
Putter, *Political Constitution of the German Empire.*
Stanhope, *War of the Spanish Succession.*
Finlay, *History of Greece.*
Rambaud, *History of Russia.*
Elphinstone, *History of India.*

1714-1815.

Lecky, *History of England in the 18th Century.*
Stanhope, *History of England.*
"   *Life of Pitt.*
Martineau, *History of England.*
Cornewall Lewis, *Essays on the Administrations of Grt. Britain.*
Alison, *Life of Castlereagh* (ch. I–III).
Bolingbroke, *Letters on History.*
"   *Dissertations on the State of Parties.*

1715-1815.

Heeren, *Political Systems of Europe.*
Martin, *Histoire de France.*
Tocqueville, *L'Ancien Régime et la Révolution.*
Von Sybel, *French Revolution.*
Taine,   "   "
Carlyle,   "   "
Lanfrey, *History of Napoleon.*
Alison, *History of Europe* (beginning with ch. LX).
Ranke, *History of Prussia.*

Bolingbroke, *Letter to Sir W. Wynd-*
   ham.
  "   *Patriot King.*
Burke, *Thoughts on Present Discon-*
   tentment.
  "   *American Taxation.*
  "   *Refl. on the French Revolution.*
  "   *Refl. on a Regicide Peace.*
Arthur Young, *Tour in England.*
Bancroft, *History of United States.*
Marshman, *History of India* (edition
   in 3 volumes).

Carlyle, *Frederick the Great.*
Frédéric II, *Mémoires.*
Seeley, *Life and Times of Stein.*
Häusser, *Deutsche Geschichte vom Tode*
   Friedrichs des Grossen.
Coxe, *Bourbon Kings in Spain.*
Napier, *Battles and Sieges in the Penin-*
   sula.
Rambaud, *History of Russia.*
Elphinstone, *History of India.*

1760-1848.

Lecky, *History of Eng. in 18th Cent.*
Stanhope, *History of England.*
  "   *Life of Pitt.*
Martineau, *History of England.*
S. Walpole,   "   "   "
Cornewall Lewis, *Essays on the Ad-*
   ministration of Grt. Britain.
Alison, *Life of Castlereagh* (ch. I–III,
   XV, XVI).
Burke, *Thoughts on Present Discontent-*
   ment.
  "   *American Taxation.*
  "   *Refl. on the French Revolution.*
  "   *Letters on a Regicide Peace.*
Samuel Baneford (principal passages
   of his life).
Nicholls, *History of the English Poor*
   Law.
Morley, *Life of Cobden.*
Bancroft, *United States.*
Payne, *History of the Colonies.*
Marshman, *History of India.*
Kaye, *Life of Metcalfe.*

1763-1848.

Heeren, *Political Systems of Modern*
   Europe.
Martin, *Histoire de France.*
Tocqueville, *Anc. Rég. et Rév.*
Arthur Young, *Travels in France.*
Von Sybel, *French Revolution.*
Mignet, *French Revolution.*
Taine,   "   "
Carlyle,   "   "
Lanfrey, *History of Napoleon.*
Guizot, *Mémoires.*
Alison, *History of the French Revolu-*
   tion (from ch. IX).
  "   *History of Europe* (from 1815).
Fyffe, *Modern History.*
Seeley, *Life and Times of Stein.*
Häusser, *D. G. vom Tode F. d. G.*
Napier, *Battles and sieges in the Penin-*
   sula.
Finlay, *History of Greece.*
Rambaud, *History of Russia.*

I shall be pardoned, I hope, for introducing here the titles
of all these works, for it seemed that nothing else would
show so well the scope of this examination. It will be observed that the list is much longer than the corresponding
list at Cambridge. As a bibliographic index it is perfect.

But is it possible for the student to read all these books?
Evidently not, for care is often taken to indicate chapters
and even the pages to be referred to. The science is thus
chalked out. But is it wise to say to the student, " Here is
a book. Read thirty or fifty pages at the beginning, in the
middle, or at the end of it?" This method seems to me
scarcely scientific. I prefer the precept of Cambridge, " Read
as many as you can of the books indicated, but read them
well and from cover to cover." Finally, does not the Oxford
list contain works somewhat superannuated?

However this may be, the student at Oxford as well as at
Cambridge is urged to read, and to read much ; in reality the
serious student does read and read much. The theoretical
course happily consumes only a small part of his day (two or
three hours), and for the rest of the time he studies at will—
to use the authorized expression, he reads. It is much to have
established advanced teaching upon such a footing. The judgment of the student is developed, independent thinking is
induced, above all, self-help must be relied on even in the
use of historical text-books.

But the Oxford examination includes also a more scientific
test—the special subject studied from the sources. In the
prospectus for 1886 I find six subjects indicated, from which
the candidates may choose. They are :

I. Hildebrand, according to Lambert de Hersfeld, Jaffé's
Monumenta Gregoriana, and Waltram's *De Unitate Ecclesiæ*.

II. The first three Crusades, from *Gesta Francorum*, Rai-
mond de Agiles, Fulcherius Carnotensis, William of Tyre
(Bk. XVI and XVII, Ch. I–VIII), *Itinerarium Regis Ri-
cardi*, and extracts from Arabian historians cited by Michaud,
Bibliothéque des Croisades.

III. Italy from 1492 to 1513, from Machiavelli (*Il Prin-
cipe*), Commines (Bk. VII and VIII), Guicciardini (*Storia
Florentina*) and Da Porto (*Lettere Storiche*). Knowledge of
Italian seems indispensable here, as these authors are referred
to in the original.

IV. The great revolution of England to the death of
Charles I (1639–1649), from Clarendon (Bk. I–VIII), the
Rushworth collection (part IV), Cromwell (Letters and
speeches, ed. Carlyle), the Long Parliament, by May, Baillie's
Letters, and Sprigg's *Anglia Rediviva.*

V. The French revolution to the end of the Convention
(1789–1795), from Rabault and Lacretelle (*Précis de la Revo-
lution Française*), Bailly (*Mémoires*, up to 14th July), the
Correspondence of Mirabeau (with Lamarck), *Mémoires* of
Bertrand de Malleville, passages selected from Girondins and
Robespierre, *Mémoires* of Madame Roland, Arthur Young's
Travels in France, and Schmidt's *Tableaux de la Révolution*
(Vol. I, Part II).

VI. History of English India from 1773 to 1805, from
Wilson (Mill's India, after Bk. V), Grant-Duff's History of
the Mahrattas, Gleig's Papers in Life of Warren Hastings,
Wilks' *Mysoor*, Cornwallis (numerous selections from his
Correspondence, referred to with the exact page), Wellesley
and Wellington (Despatches, ed. Owen).

I heartily approve the principle of this test, but I question
whether the subjects involved are not too vast. How can a
student bound to prepare a multitude of other subjects read
with any degree of seriousness the documents of the French
Revolution from 1789 to the end of the Convention? The
same may be asked of the other subjects. Such study of
sources is of necessity superficial; it must be restricted, in
my opinion, to a brief and scarcely reliable verification of
what the standard authors assert. Fortunately, the student
is not absolutely bound to this list of topics that I have called
too vast. He is permitted to choose for himself a special
subject, provided he make arrangement with the Faculty six
months before the examination. His request must be accompanied by a list of the books and documents he purposes to
use. But this privilege the students almost never avail themselves of, and, if I mistake not, will neglect no less in the
future. It would be better to restrict the topics so as to

In his course at the university he explained English Charters and laws of the Middle Ages. The students took notes,
which the professor would at request inspect. Out of seventy
auditors in 1884, a dozen gave their note-books to the professor, who took the trouble to correct them carefully. His
object was to rouse in his pupils a critical spirit with regard
to the study of original sources without any direct application
to politics. His method tended to form scholars, not future
statesmen, and no one could pretend to guide better than he
to disinterested and scientific historical erudition.

Not finding at Oxford a practical course in history, the
students recently took it upon themselves to supply the want.
The idea had its birth in the brain of an American, Mr.
Brearley. He had, before entering Balliol College, Oxford,
spent some years in Germany as tutor to American students
and had heard of the historical seminaries there, without
having admission to them. At Oxford he found no such
institution. He related what he had heard of it in Germany,
gained the coöperation of his fellows and founded in 1882 the
" Historical Seminary," numbering at the time only fifteen
members, and in 1884 thirty-five—an average of two to each
college. They hold three or four meetings in a term, lasting
from eight to ten o'clock in the evening. After one of the
members has read a paper of which the hearers take notes,
five or six who have read up the same subject then debate the
question with the leader. Sometimes the discussion becomes
very earnest. The presidency is given, not to a student, but
to a professor, formerly to Mr. Stubbs or, if convenient, to
Mr. Bright or another lecturer as a substitute. The presi-
dent calls attention to the defects of the paper read and gives
the résumé at the close of the debate. At one time the
argument was prolonged till midnight, the question under
discussion being the High Church of the seventeenth century.
The meetings are held in the studies of the various members,
the one who entertains furnishing coffee, tea and cigarettes.

The subjects of discussion always bear upon the matter of

the examinations. The members receive at the beginning of each term a printed program, so that each one may, if he chooses, seriously prepare for the debate. Below is the list for the Summer term of 1884 : I. Monday, 28 April, Thesis by Mr. J. Wells on the influence of France upon the politics and social life of England during the reign of Charles II. II. Monday, 12 May, Thesis by Mr. H. Hutton upon William III. III. Monday, 26 May, Thesis by Mr. G. Saunders upon the campaigns of Marlborough.

I regretted extremely the impossibility of attending one of these meetings ; for the novel institution greatly interested me on account both of the original style of its establishment and of the good grace with which the venerable Mr. Stubbs and his colleagues followed the lead of their pupils in supplying the desideratum at Oxford.

Lately a second historical club has been formed there, named the Stubbs Club, where theses on English History are read. At Christ Church College, too, there is a small historical society. In the Oxford Magazine for 25th February, 1885, I read that the club met in the study of one of its members and that a paper was read upon the deposition of Edward II, of Richard II and of Henry VI, seven members taking part in the discussion.

The Historical Seminary devotes itself to the study of modern History ; its success suggested to students of the classics the founding of an Ancient History Seminary. By this time it must be in full operation as it had been definitely projected in April, 1884. I said above that ancient history was united with study of the classics. Surely students of this class will find it pleasant to be organized into a historical seminary and thus to emerge from the seclusion that has hitherto weighed upon the history student of scientific aims at Oxford.

Another institution, already old, contributes much to encourage the study of history. I refer to the prizes offered to students or graduates, for the best essay upon given topics.

There are at least three prizes each year at Oxford: the Stanhope prize for a subject in modern history is restricted to undergraduates; the two others are especially sought by the graduates; the Lothian prize is also for modern history, while the Arnold prize is given alternately to ancient and modern history. There is also an annual prize, appointed by the chancellor of the university—sometimes for a historical subject. The topics for the prize essays are given out a year in advance. Judges are chosen from the professors and other dignitaries. Professors and lecturers stand ready to give the aspirants all advice and references, but they can have no further knowledge of the essays which are sent anonymously to the judges. Usually there are many contestants—for the Stanhope prize sometimes forty. The prizes are of some value: £20 for the Stanhope essay, £40 for the Lothian, and £42 for the Arnold essay. These contests are perquisites of the ablest students, furnishing opportunity for individual work and tempting them to prolong their stay at the university and their pursuit of history. Mr. Stubbs and several of his colleagues spoke to me with enthusiasm of this style of encouragement, and I agreed with them in view of the very substantial results it has produced. Mr. Stubbs, who was naturally one of the judges in 1884, assured me that for the Stanhope prize—History of Montenegro—he had received among the eleven essays offered, drawn from original Slavic as well as Latin sources, several of solid merit, filling when printed no less than two hundred pages. For the Lothian prize—The Art of War in the Middle Ages—were written four voluminous papers, and for the Arnold prize—Life of the Chancellor Thomas More—six of equal merit. Mr. Stubbs pronounced the successful essays works of real value.

This statement I could easily credit, as I had seen some of the essays, and among them the one that took the Lothian prize in 1882, a truly remarkable paper. It was "James and Philip van Artevelde," by Mr. W. J. Ashley, B. A., former scholar of Balliol College, whom I met at Oxford. This

young savant, a man of great promise, was then a candidate
for the chair of history in a school of high grade in Wales.
According to custom his application was accompanied by certificates from specialists, among whom were Mr. Stubbs and
my compatriot Mr. Léon Vanderkindere, professor at the free
university of Brussels and author of *Le Siècle des Artevelde.* In
addition Mr. Ashley sent flattering testimonials from former
pupils, among which were two from young ladies. All these
certificates, prepared for the officials in charge of the nomina-
tion, were bound in a pamphlet and accompanied by reviews
of his book taken from the *Pall Mall Gazette, Saturday Review,
Contemporary Review,* the *Guardian* and the *Literary World.* I
may notice here in passing, as related to my subject, this novel
manner, at once scientific and practical, of applying for a
vacant chair. Each candidate follows the same course and
thus their various claims are publicly submitted to competent
judges. It seems to me it would be well to introduce this
custom on the Continent.

I am happy to greet in Mr. Ashley a brilliant disciple of
Oxford's historical methods. He won in 1881 first rank in
the history examination, and his prize essay of the following year marks the excellence of the method he has followed,
showing that though Oxford still lacks a practical course, the
prize-system, for the chosen few at least, supplies the deficiency.

Another encouragement to original research is found in the
newly established historical society at Oxford, devoted to local
history and the history of the university, and purposing to
publish its most interesting documents. Here a vast field is
opened to young investigators, furnishing immediately at hand
abundant and well-defined materials.

I ought here to thank Mr. Stubbs for his extremely kind
reception of me at Oxford. Although he was on the point
of departure, he put himself at my disposal, graciously furnishing me the information I asked, and permitting me to note
down his replies. The venerable man, like Prof. Beets, of
Utrecht, the great writer of Holland, seemed to me the per-

sonification of his serene science.   In him Oxford loses much.
I wish also to thank Mr. Lodge and Mr. George for the many
useful hints which they have given me, by no means forgetting
my excellent friend, Mr. Charles H. Firth, correspondent of
the *Revue historique* of Paris.

V.—Historical Instruction in London.

When the traveller leaves Cambridge and Oxford, where
the universities with their splendid Gothic architecture con-
stitute the town, for London, the busy metropolis, he finds it
difficult to discover there the seat of learning, so small are
its pretensions.   Moreover, the University of London, which
occupies a palace in the rear of the Art Academy, is not a
university.   It is only fine quarters, where twice a year examinations are held for degrees in philosophy, literature, sciences,
law and medicine, before a board of examiners appointed by
the State.   The instructing is done in several private estab-
lishments called colleges, the principal ones being University
College and King's College; both of these are almost universities in the Continental sense.

Founded in 1828, chiefly by the efforts of Lord Brougham,
University College is open to all sects; consequently its teaching is unsectarian.   To offset this liberality, the partisans of
the Anglican Church established King's College, where each
day opens with prayers at which all students must be present.
The State does not directly support either of these institutions,
but it favors the latter by granting its very desirable site in
the Strand.   In other respects the two colleges are entirely
independent.

History plays but a secondary part and boasts but one
professor in each institution.   In University College, Mr. E.
S. Beesly, one of the most distinguished of English positivists,
teaches general, ancient, mediæval, modern, and contemporary
history.   In 1883–1884, he devoted to these subjects one hour
a week, on Thursdays.   Of these, ten lectures were given to

Roman history, from the death of Sulla to that of Cæsar;
fifteen to tracing in broad outline the history of Europe from
the close of the Middle Ages to our own day.   In accordance
with the positivist doctrine, the program was inscribed " The
object of this course is to represent the history of the West as
a continuous and natural evolution."[1]   About twenty-five
students attended Mr. Beesly's course.

At King's College there is a professor of modern history,
Mr. S. R. Gardiner, whose books are deservedly well known,
and a lecturer, Mr. Sidney J. M. Low;[2] the latter has charge
of the first year pupils.   He teaches them general English
history up to the end of the seventeenth century.   Mr. Gardiner provides a more advanced course, embracing only a shorter
period of national history, usually about fifty years, which he
presents in detail.   Ancient history is joined with the classics.

Mr. Gardiner's lectures, one of which I attended, take an
hour and a quarter twice a week.   The professor and students
are dressed in their black gowns, their square caps laid on the
desk beside their note-books.   Before the lecture an officer
carefully calls the roll—a formality not observed at University College, where attendance is not compulsory.   There
were twelve students present at the lecture I attended.   Mr.
Gardiner's subject was the state of the English Church under
Queen Elizabeth.   He spoke simply and clearly, without
attempt at eloquence, reminding me of a German professor,
the resemblance being heightened, no doubt, by the somewhat
Teutonic cast of the professor's features and his expression of
learned candor and almost anxious good will.   From time to
time he readjusted his eyeglasses and polished his nose with
his large colored handkerchief, like Droysen of Berlin.   He
related quietly and clearly and without euphemism the history of the dissolute clergy of the sixteenth century, especially

---

[1] See prospectus of University College, London, Session 1883–1884, pp.
18 and 19.

[2] See prospectus of King's College, London, 1883–1884, pp. 10 and 11.

4

in Great Britain. The five hearers in the first row of seats took notes most conscientiously and some of the others listened attentively; but those behind seemed occupied with other matters and eager for the lecture to close; they were little pleased when explanations detained Mr. Gardiner beyond the allotted time. In a word the audience was a mixed one. Mr. Gardiner gave very detailed and interesting explanations, but without referring his pupils to books or documents.

I have been told that the men of the London colleges are younger and not so well prepared as for Oxford and Cambridge. They appear to be collegians rather than true students. At King's College they are treated like students of a middle, not an advanced, grade. For instance, at the end of each term they have to pass an easy written examination and the first in rank receives a book as a reward of merit. There is for history a more important incentive, a scholarship of £40, awarded yearly at the Easter examination. The test consists of two essays upon periods of history previously appointed. In 1884 the subjects were: for English history, the period from 1603 to 1649, and for Continental history the corresponding period from 1610 to 1648. If two contestants are equally deserving, the scholarship is divided between them.

I wish to thank Mr. Gardiner and Mr. Beesly for the kind reception they accorded me.

VI.—CONCLUSION.

So far as I can judge, advanced instruction in history is still in an embryonic state in London, a condition not shared by Cambridge and Oxford. The Scottish universities with their almost utter poverty in the science are still farther behind than the London colleges. The interest of my investigations has therefore centred in Cambridge and Oxford. I have risked wearying the reader by giving so detailed an account of the examinations at these two universities; I will add but a few general observations.

The strain upon memory, implied by the number of books prescribed and the questions given, is appalling. The reading required is of so vast extent that the student cannot thoroughly grasp any part of it; but the correction is doubtless found in the English tradition that the pupil will assimilate to himself, chiefly by his own reading, material enough to meet the tremendous examinations. It is evident he can only skim so many vast subjects; but at least he must work almost entirely by himself.

Quite otherwise is it with the Belgian student. He is catechised by his professor on the course followed during the year, which he is supposed to know by heart, having taken care never to refer to a book and contented with the confused and misspelled notes hurriedly taken at the lecture. Only the few students of the practical course ever take in their hands the necessary books and documents.

No one would accuse the students of Cambridge and Oxford of using too few books; but are they sufficiently familiar with sources of history and original documents? I think not. It has been well said that although it is dangerous to begin *Quellenstudien* too early, as yet no better method of making historians has been discovered than that of studying sources; for the simple reason that no better method exists.[1] While it is unwise to begin this study too soon, still, until the student has been brought face to face with documents apparently contradictory which he must criticize and account for, he can have no idea of scientific structure of history. Perhaps some gifted minds can train themselves after leaving the university; but how much time spent in groping, the princes of the science would save them! How many lamentable defects mar the work of self-taught scholars, notwithstanding their genius!

[1] I cannot forbear referring my readers to the interesting monograph entitled Methods of Historical Study, by Mr. Herbert B. Adams, professor at Johns Hopkins University, Baltimore. The author states and discusses the systems successively employed in Europe (Germany, France, Belgium) and in America (especially at Johns Hopkins and Harvard Universities).

The Oxford students expressed their appreciation of this fact when they introduced the German historical seminaries.

But these seminaries differ essentially from the German. In the latter one evening's summary discussion of a subject does not suffice; documents are scrupulously dissected, one or two at a time, to extract all that each one can furnish. They are the small stones, which will go with many fellows to build up an exhaustive treatise, the work of several months. The Oxford students thus, in attempting to introduce the German method, have not begun in the right way. While I would be the last to disparage the alluring debating club where coffee and cigarettes add their charm to the hour, yet I do not hesitate to say that it cannot take the place of a practical course in a historical laboratory.

In the English universities there is also need of certain important courses preparatory for truly scientific research, such as paleography, diplomatics, and chronology. At the German universities, at the School of Charters, and at the Practical School of Higher Studies at Paris, there are experienced and enthusiastic masters in these special sciences, without which no historian can be accurate.[1]

England spends yearly sums unequalled on the continent for printing luxuriously her charters, chronicles and all sources of history, and similar publications appear for all the sciences relating to history. Of what use is this vast expense? No doubt there is in Great Britain a considerable number of scholars' and writers to whom these fine collections are valuable; but do the universities receive any benefit from them? In Germany the *Monumenta* of Pertz, the *Reichstags-akten* and all similar publications are diligently explored each year by a multitude of masters and pupils enamoured of historical research and applying to the pursuit the strictest

---

[1] I am glad to see that Mr. Burrows, professor at Oxford, in his lecture before referred to, breaks a lance in favor of the introduction of paleography among the subjects at his university.

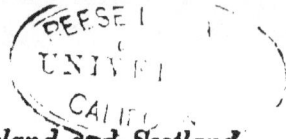

laboratory methods. The system has no parallel in the country on whose bounty it thrives. I have seen Mr. Châtelain, lecturer at *L'École pratique des hautes études* in Paris, draw for his course in paleography upon the admirable productions of the London Paleographic Society. At German universities, in German books, one continually sees the effects of "State Papers," the collections of the Camden Society and the various other documents of the kind which England scatters broadcast every year. I hope the day is not far distant when Oxford and Cambridge will count among their two hundred or their forty students of history, a chosen few who will dissect with patriotic ardor the original documents of their national history.

The remarkable development in historical instruction that has taken place at Oxford since 1870, and at Cambridge since 1875, leads one to think that the practical course will soon be felt a necessary complement to the already brilliant theoretical course. A corps at Cambridge of one professor and five lecturers for history alone or at Oxford of two professors and fourteen lecturers offers ample accommodation, at least unsurpassed by German universities. Mr. Seeley has already started along the right road. His conversation-class, though dealing with philosophical principles of history instead of with documents, is really a practical course, an intellectual dissecting-room. His skill, thought and experience are all at the disposal of the pupils who choose to be initiated in the methods of political science; there is a continual exchange between master and pupils, a Socratic, experimental system that cannot be replaced by any amount of theory. If I might counsel the five colleges at Cambridge, I should urge them each for its own specialty to follow this example—as, indeed, Mr. Browning has already done in his Political Society.

As for Oxford, I imagine that Mr. E. A. Freeman, successor to Mr. Stubbs, will of necessity be an apostle of the new school. I met him at Edinburgh, already familiar with his works, in which are reflected his vast learning, youthful spirit, originality of thought and style, and indomitable zeal in the pursuit of historical truth. So deep-dyed a historian cannot fail to exercise a direct scientific influence upon the young men thronging to him, and no doubt circumstances will aid him. That the change is brewing at Oxford is proved by the establishment of the two seminaries and the other historical circles. The younger lecturers with whom I have spoken are already enlisted in the cause. The fruit is ripe and will soon fall.[1]

Advanced historical instruction in England to-day rivals that of Germany and Paris; and every year the English universities produce new pioneers, eager and well-equipped, bringing to history the clear-sightedness and sound judgment that characterizes all Anglo-Saxon science. The continually increasing number of prizes and fellowships (for England is the home of intelligent endowments), positive encouragements with which the Continent is not familiar, peculiarly favor the progress of disinterested research, and keep from want those devotees who, like the brave *privat-docenten* of Germany, give their lives to their cause without one ray of promised remuneration.

---

[1] In his opening lecture before referred to, Mr. Freeman lets it appear what will be his tendency at Oxford.